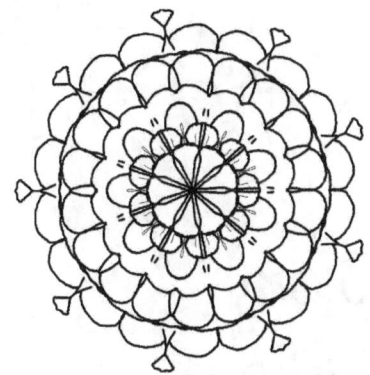

Colour Me Happy

By: Yesha Shah

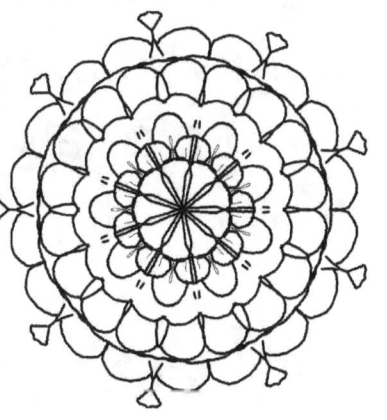

Living in the world of technology, sometimes we just need to create an environment for ourselves to unplug, relax and indulge in a non-screen related activity. Grab some coloured pens, pencils or markers and color away the floral manadalas and symmetrical tiles.

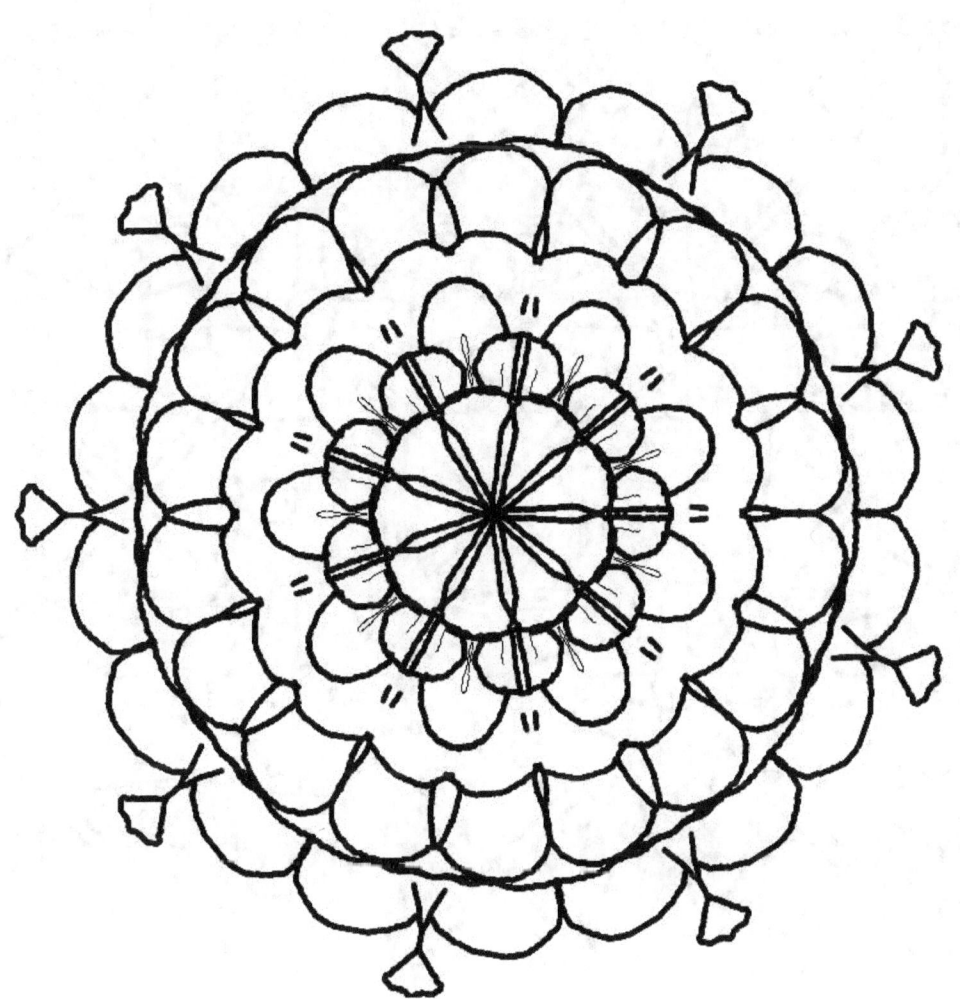

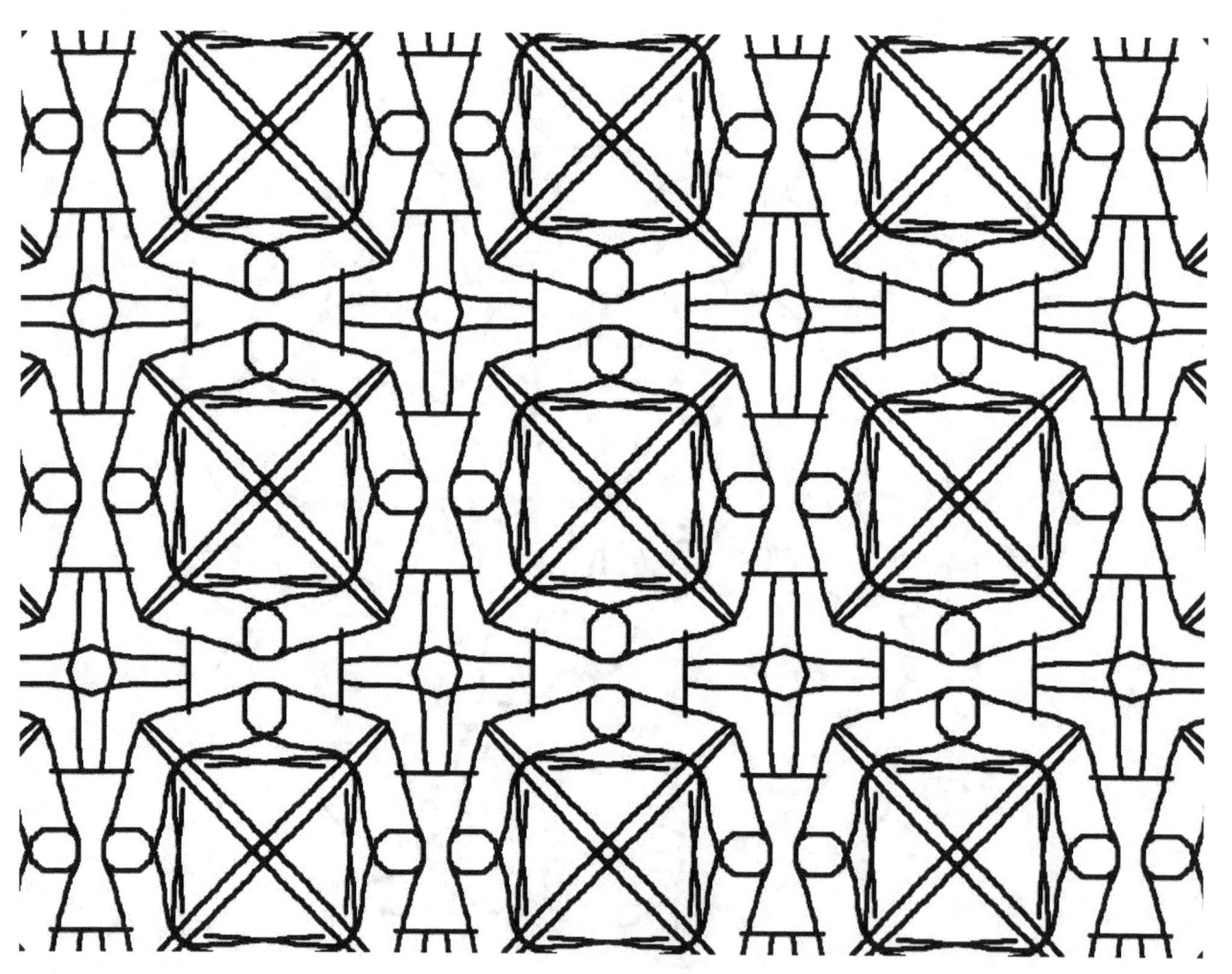

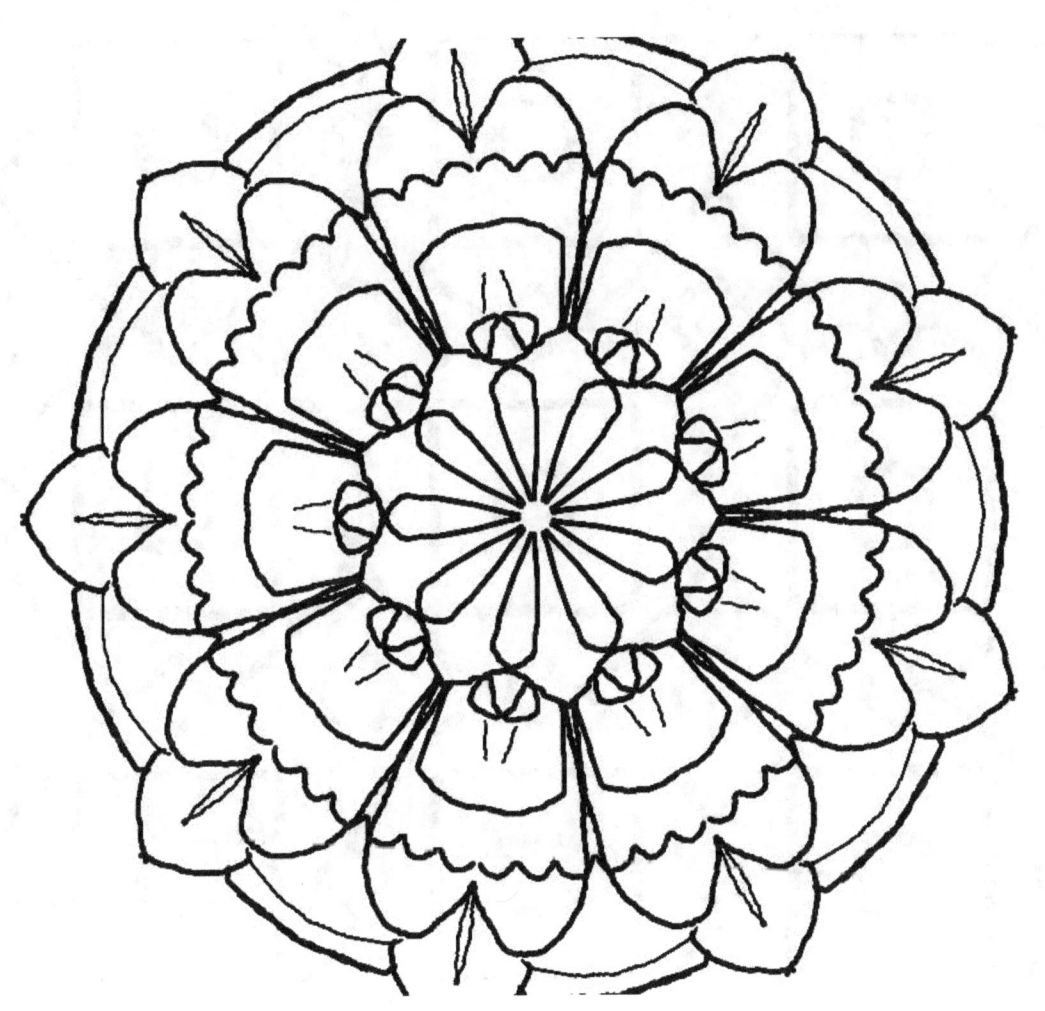

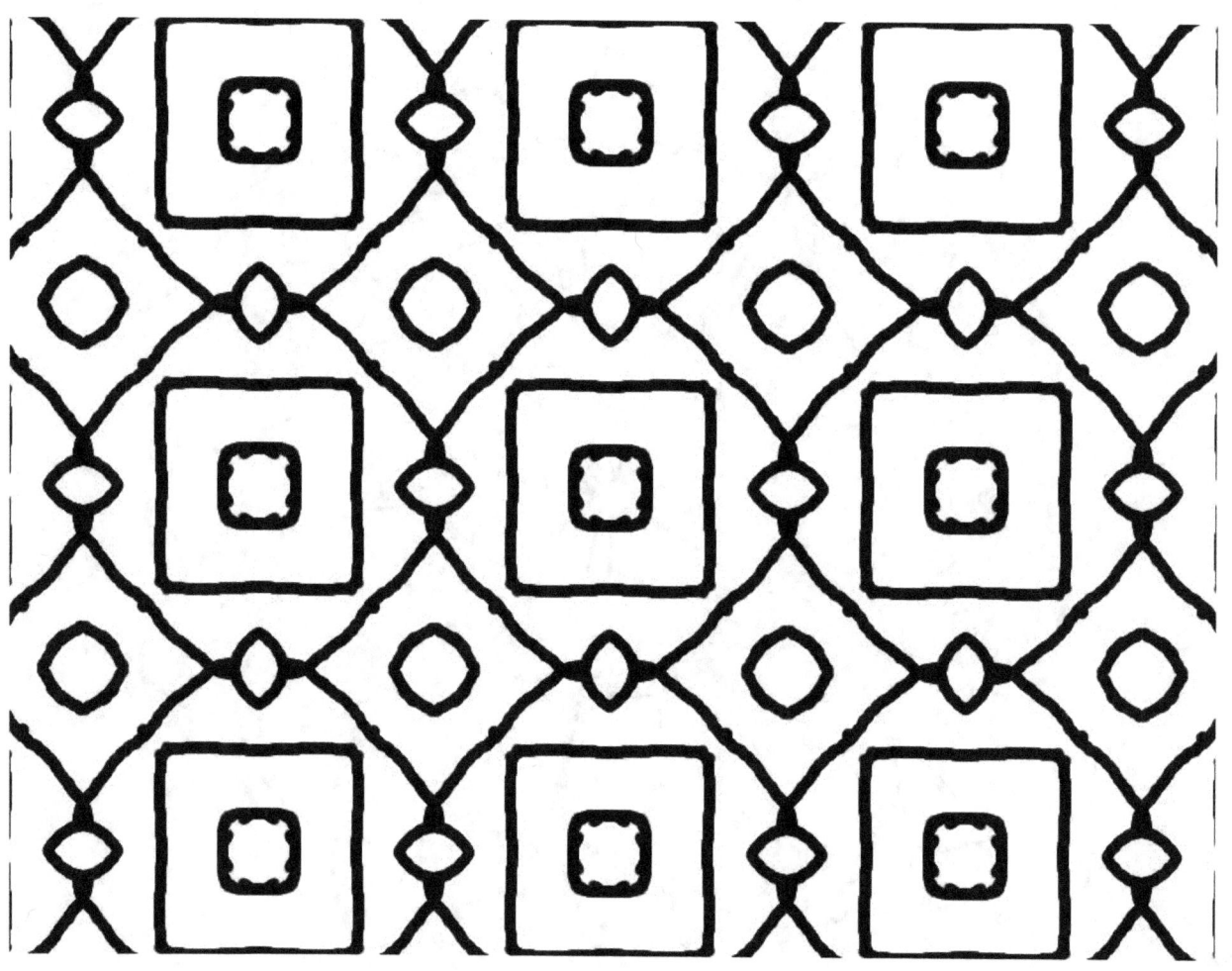

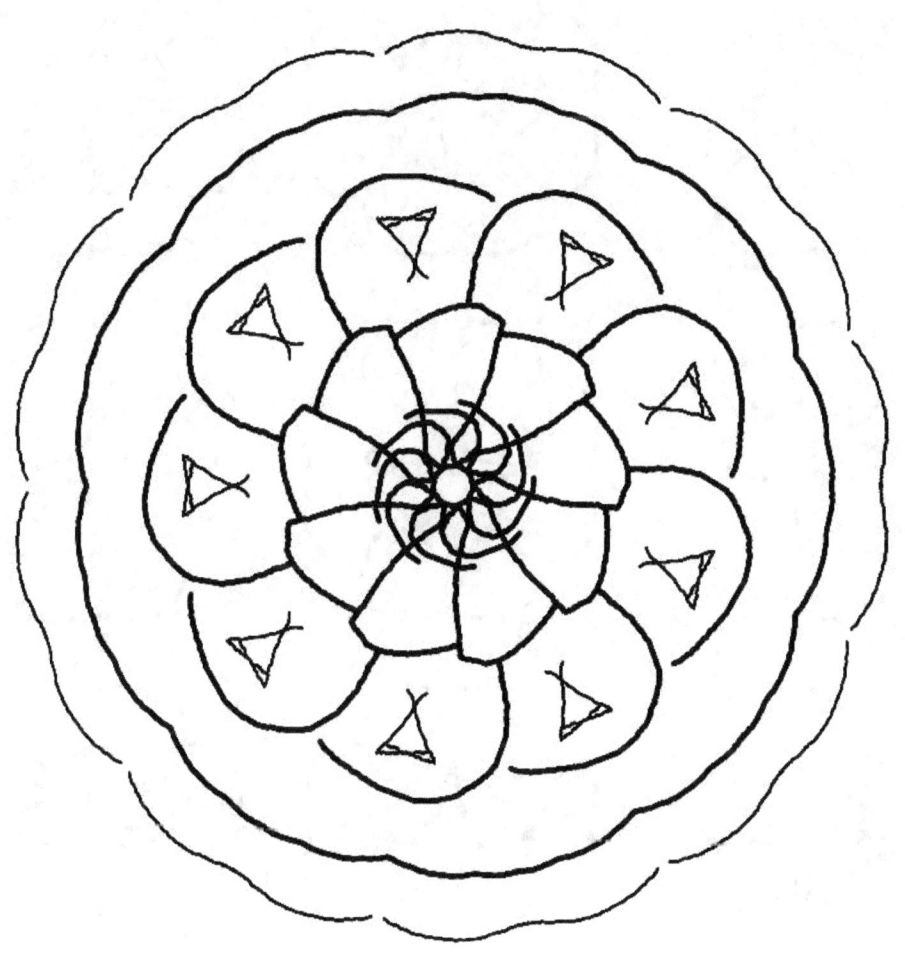

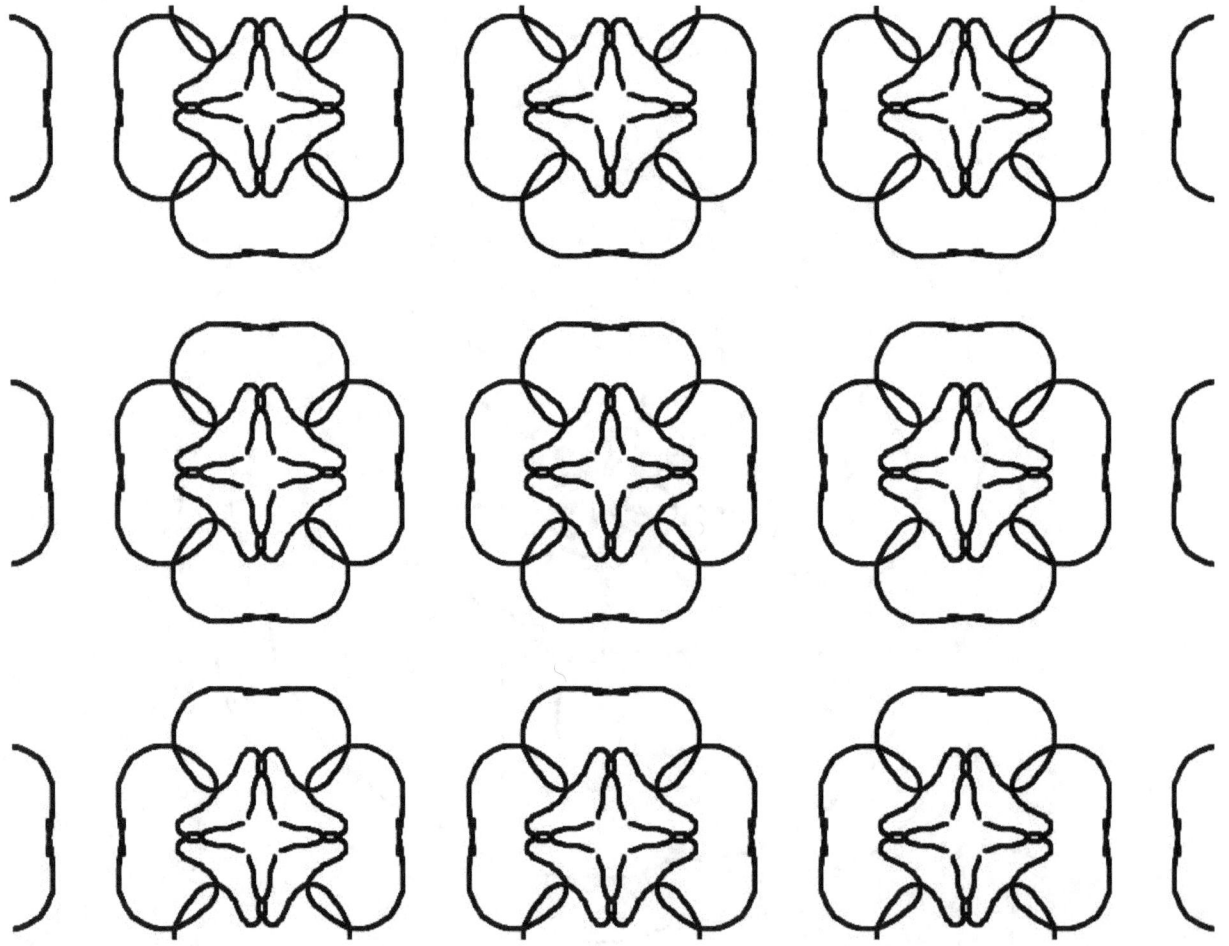

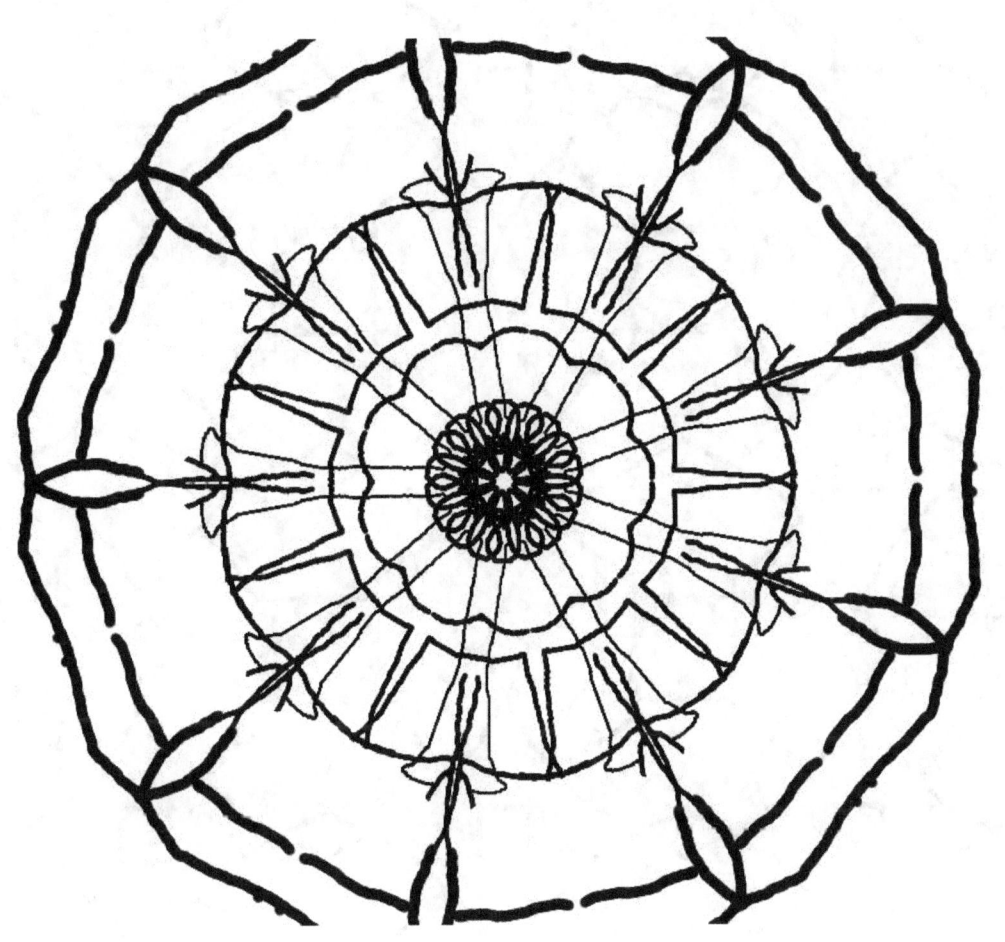

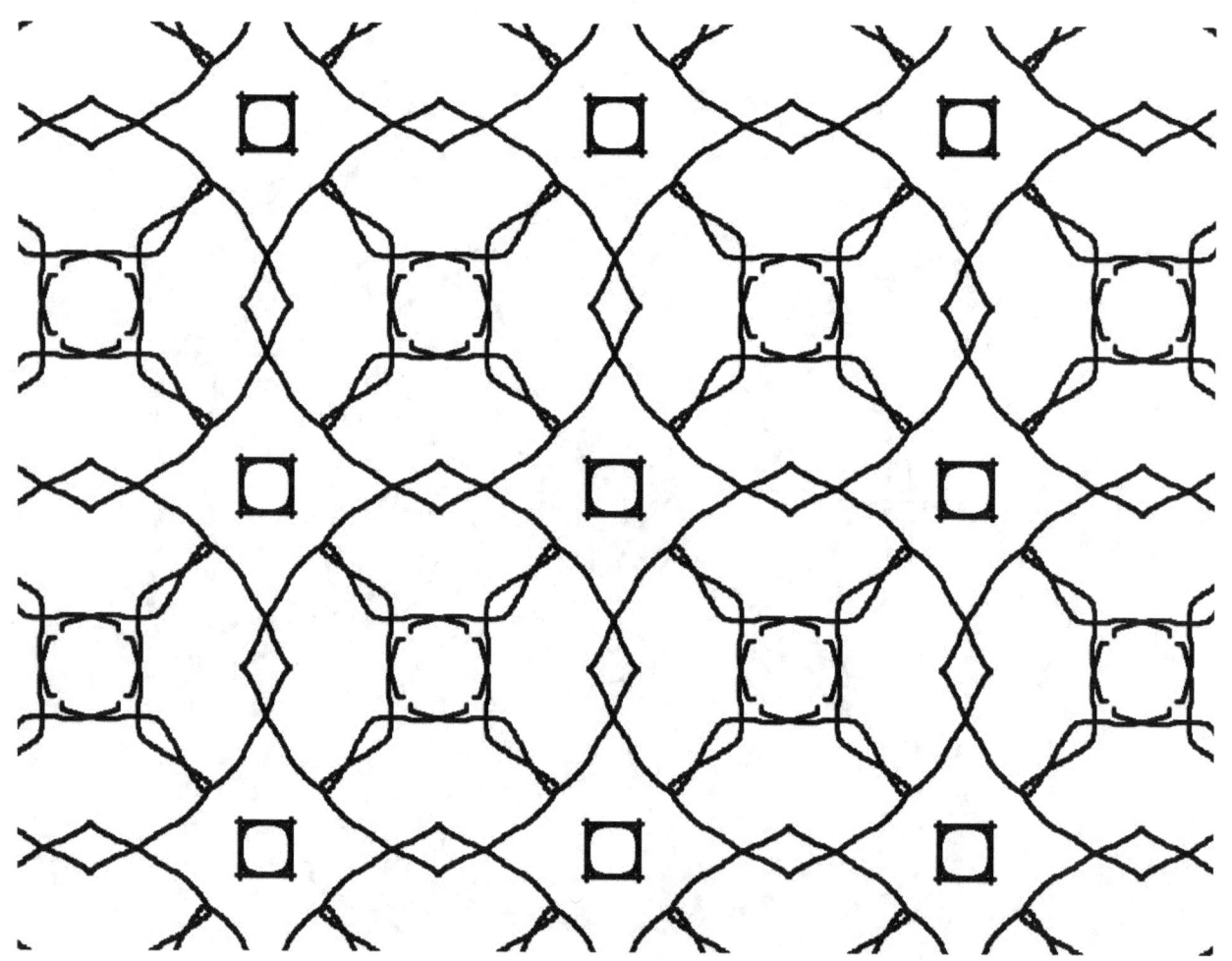

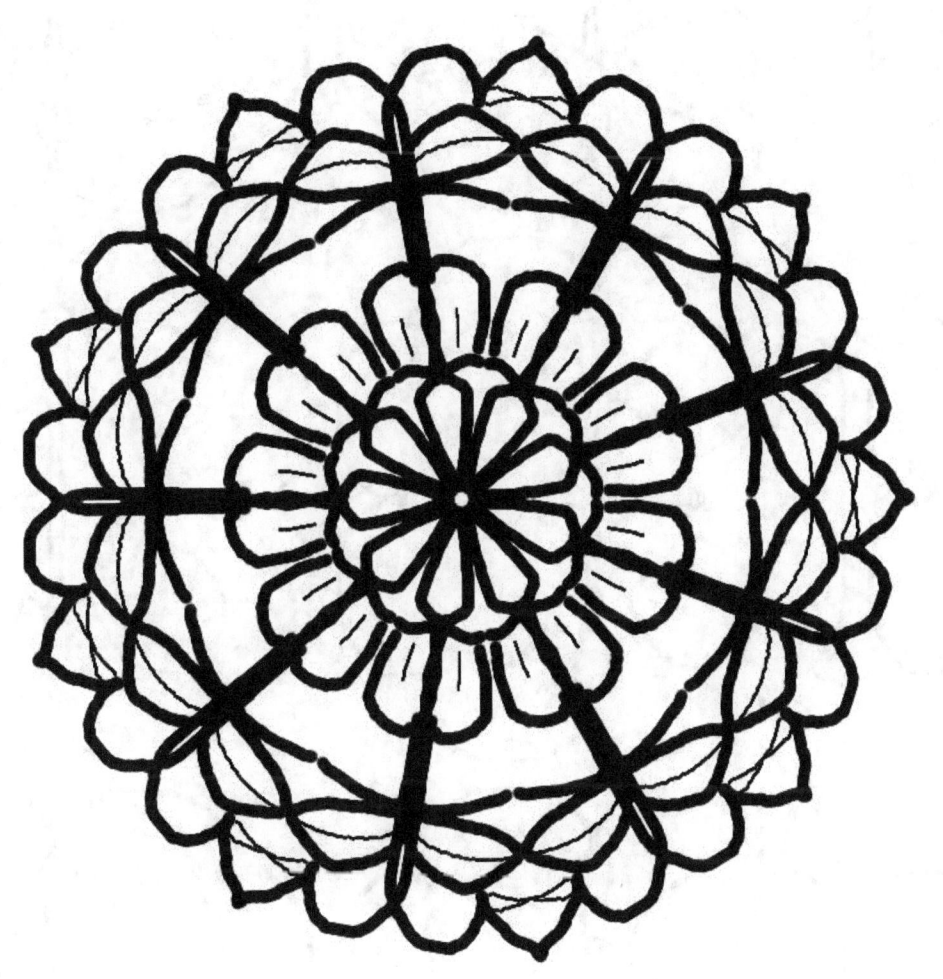

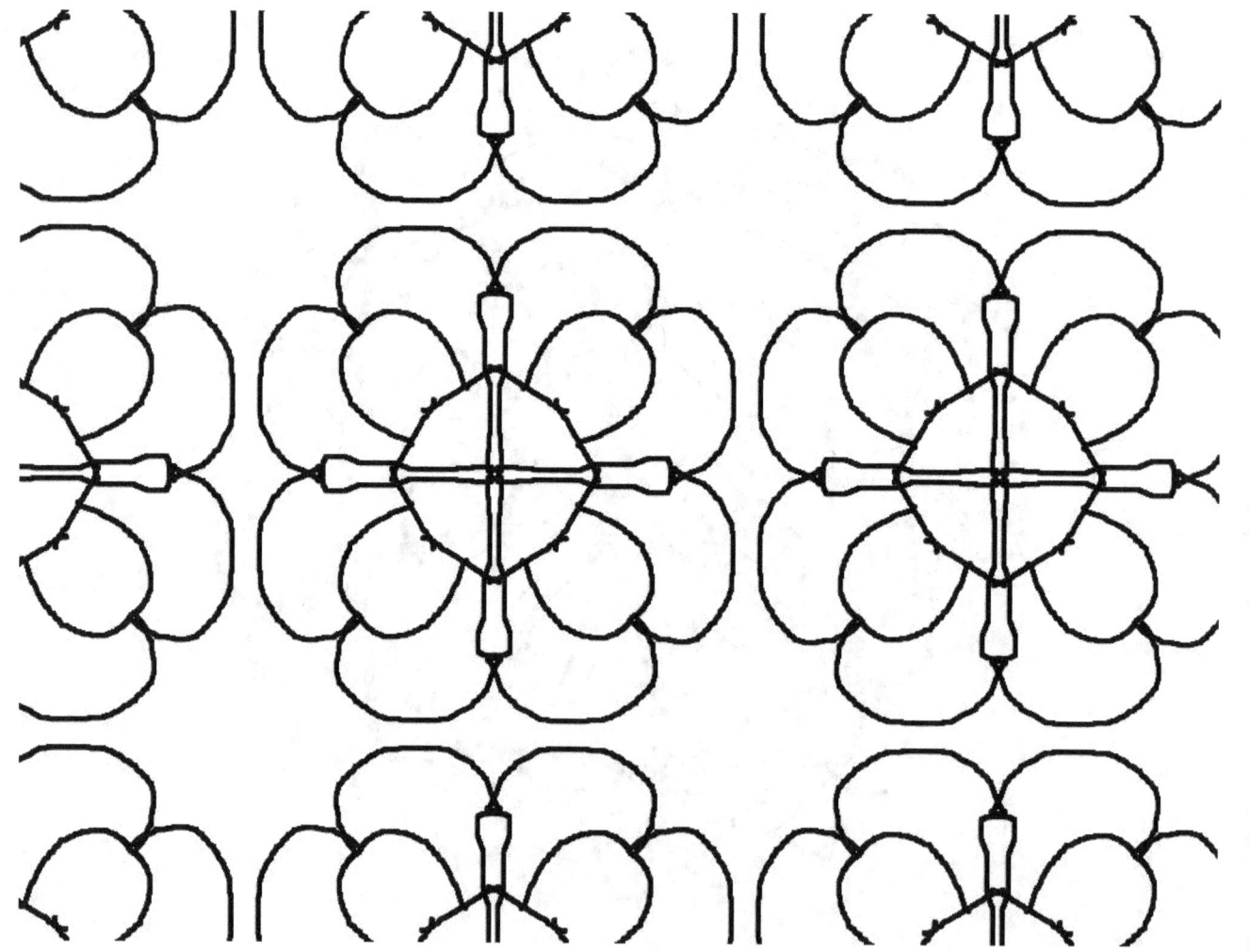

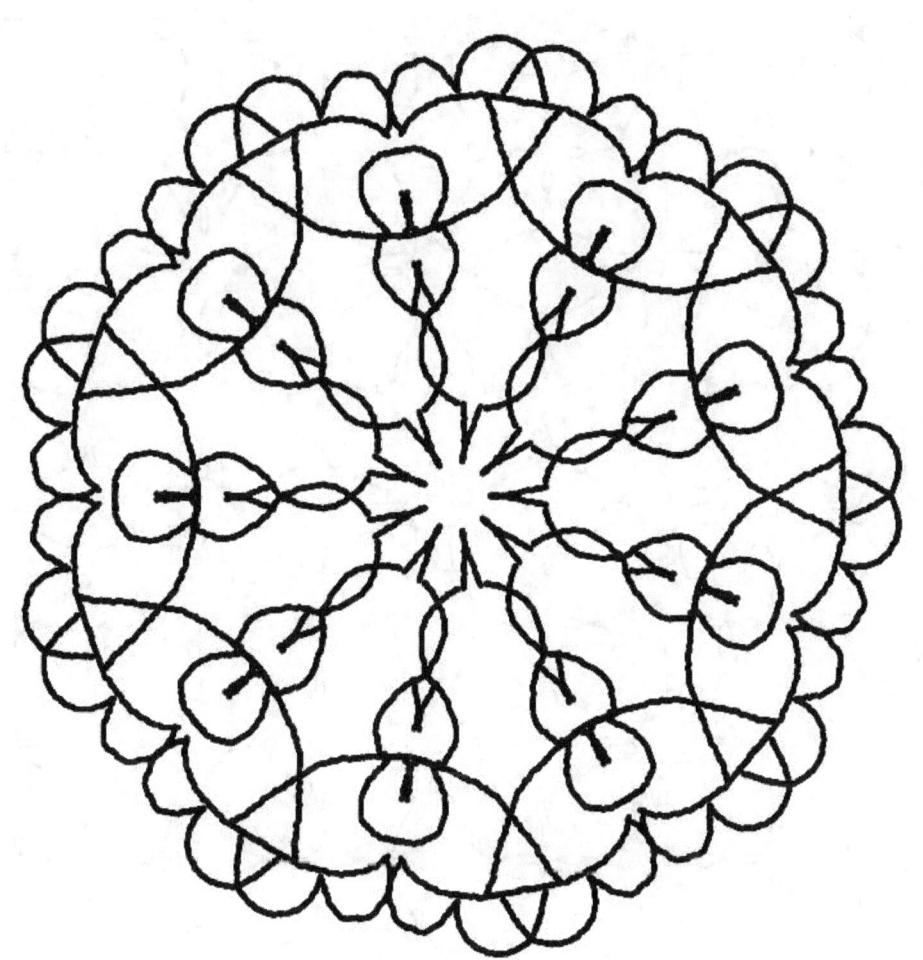

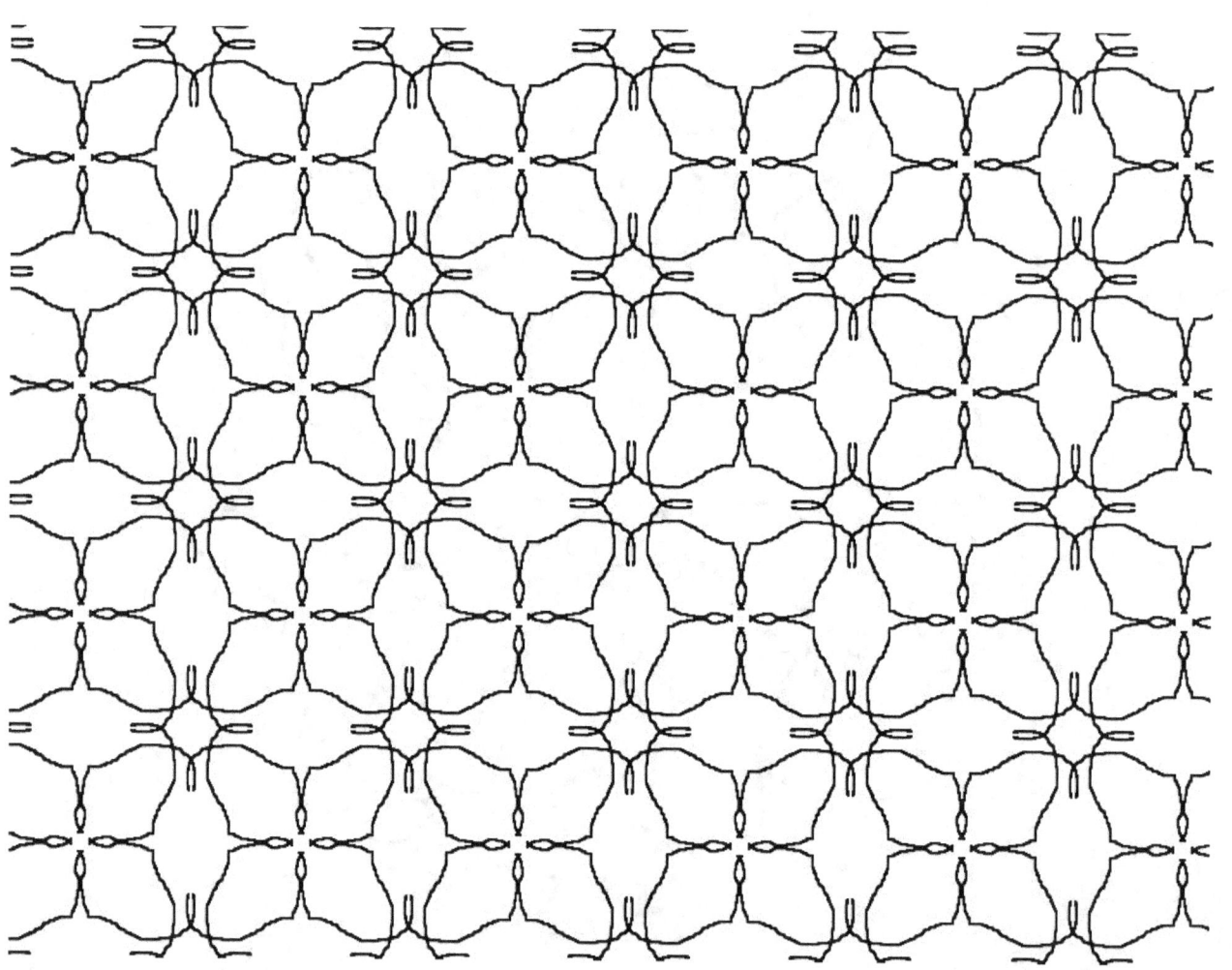

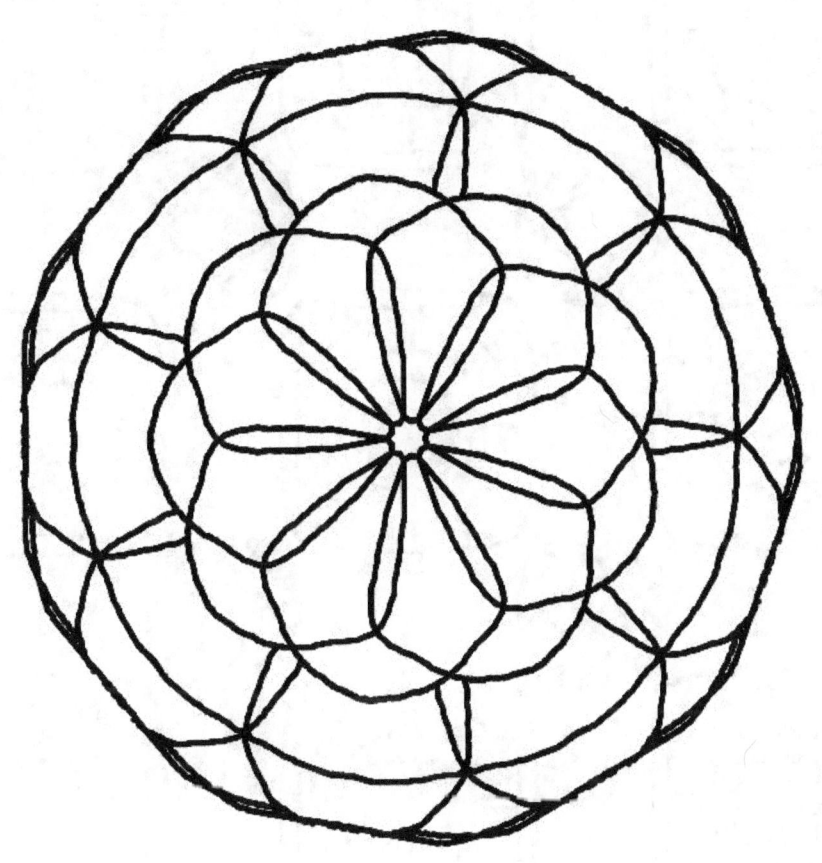

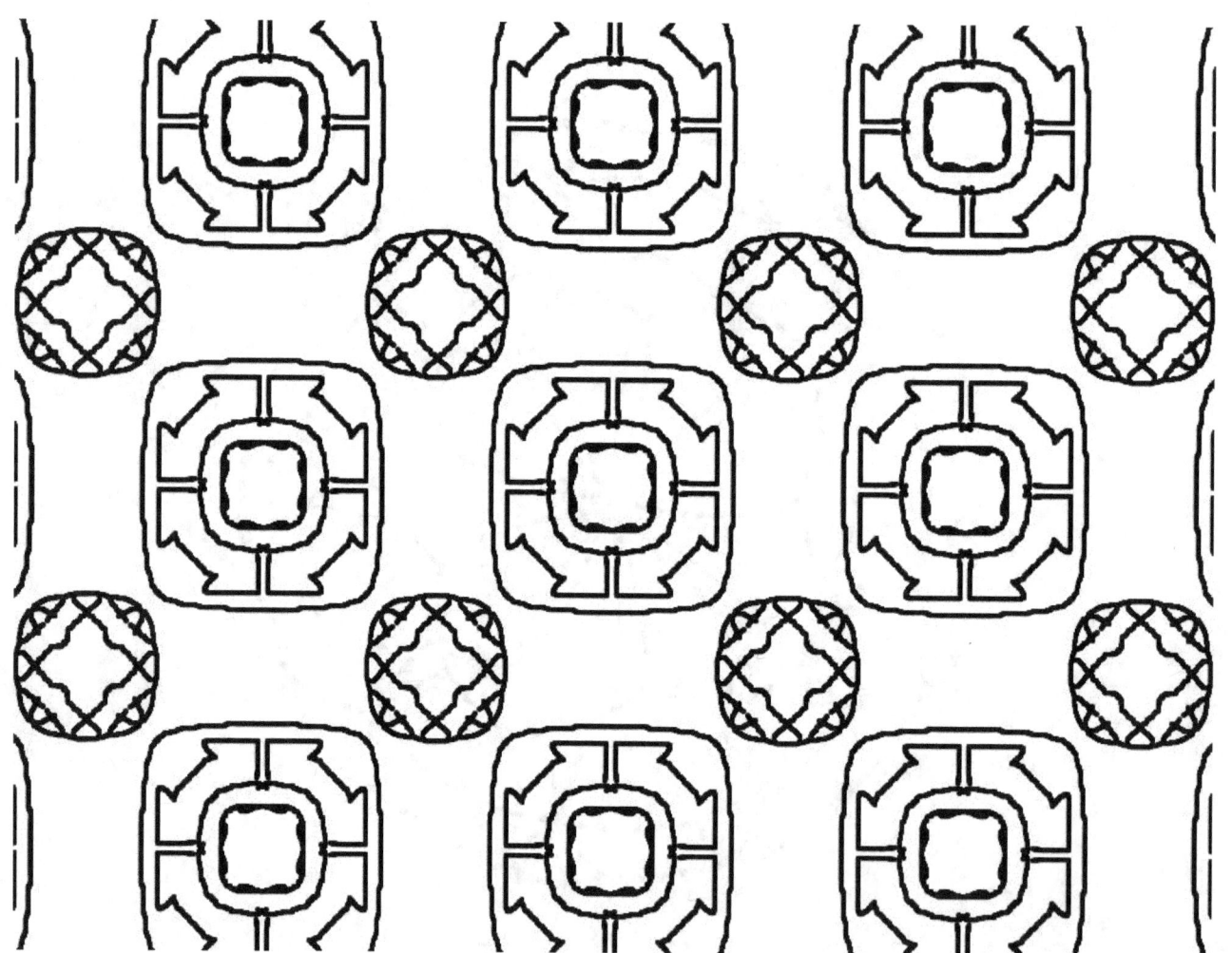

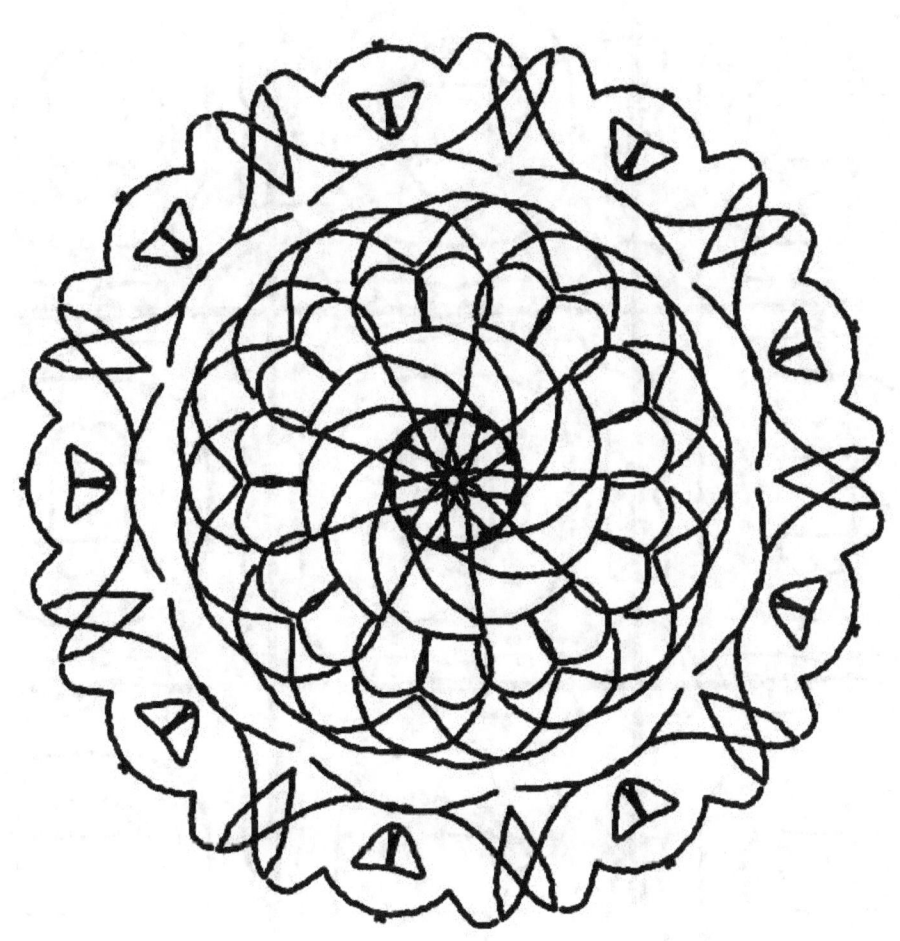

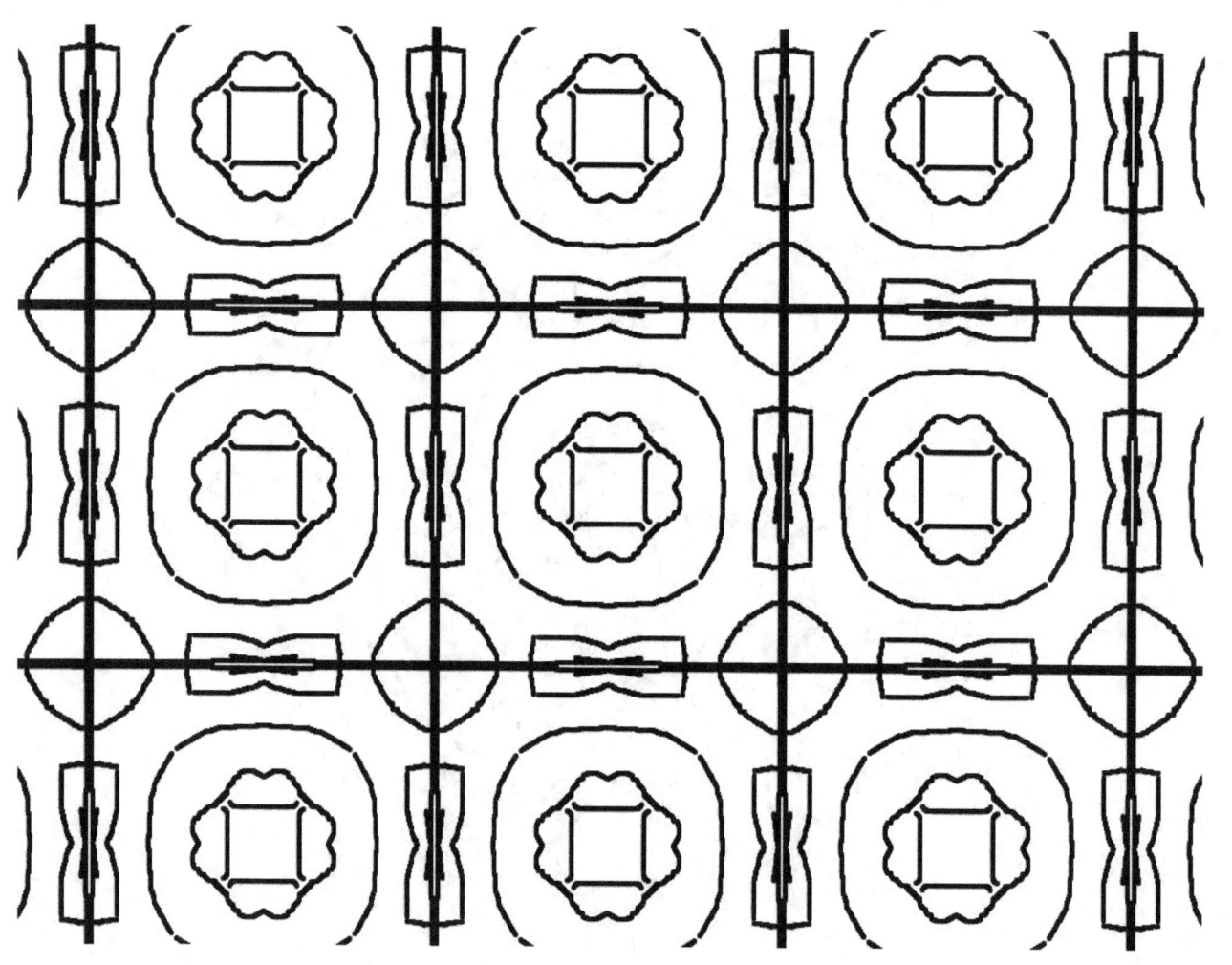

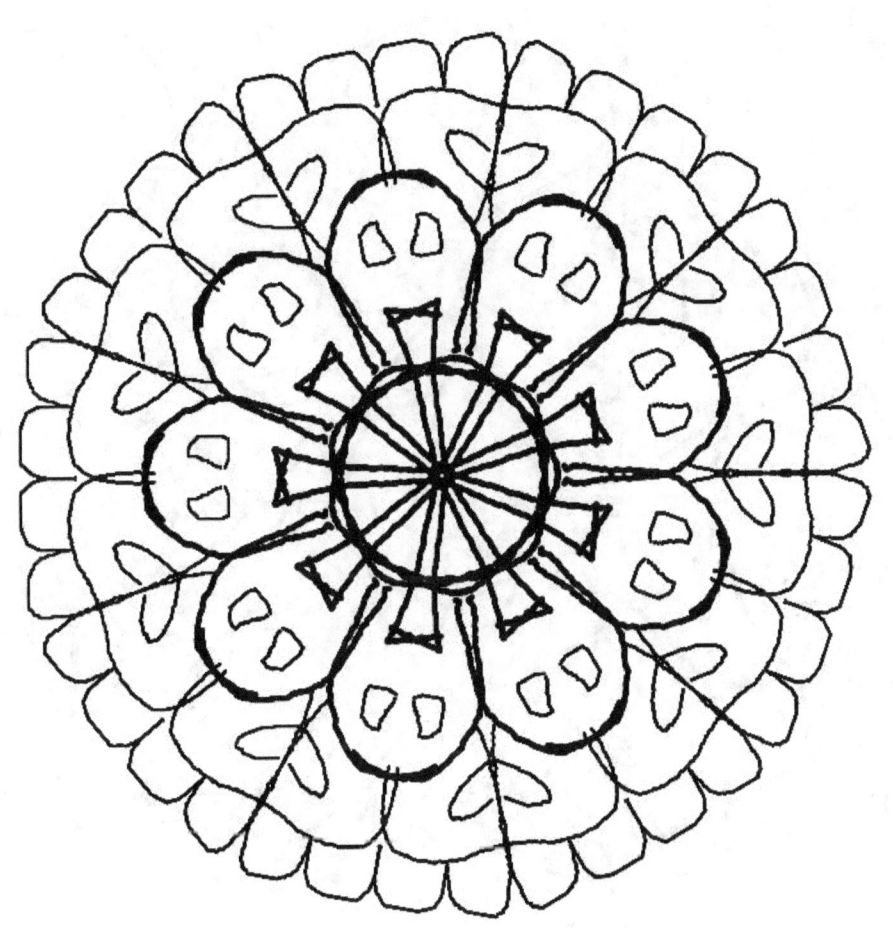

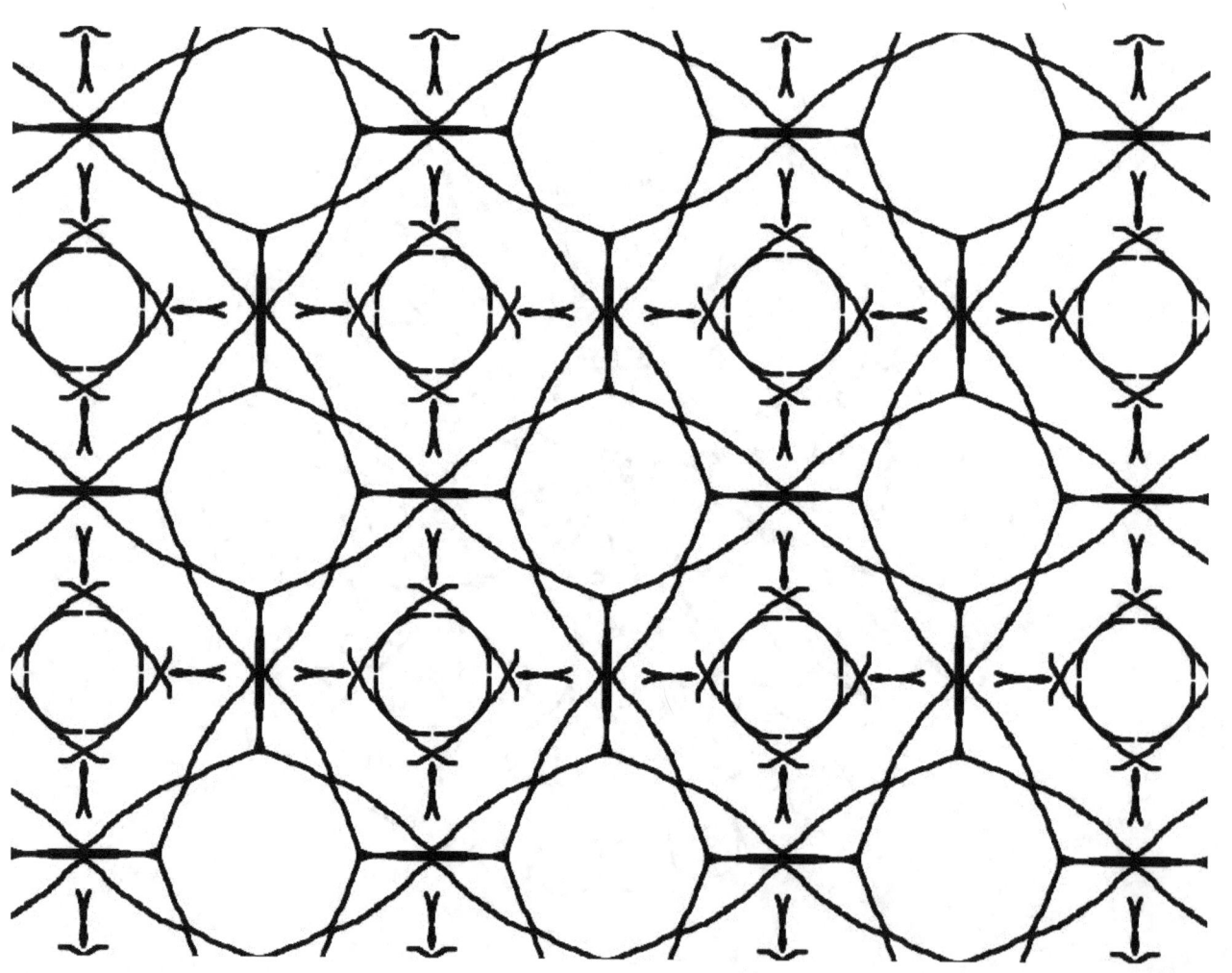

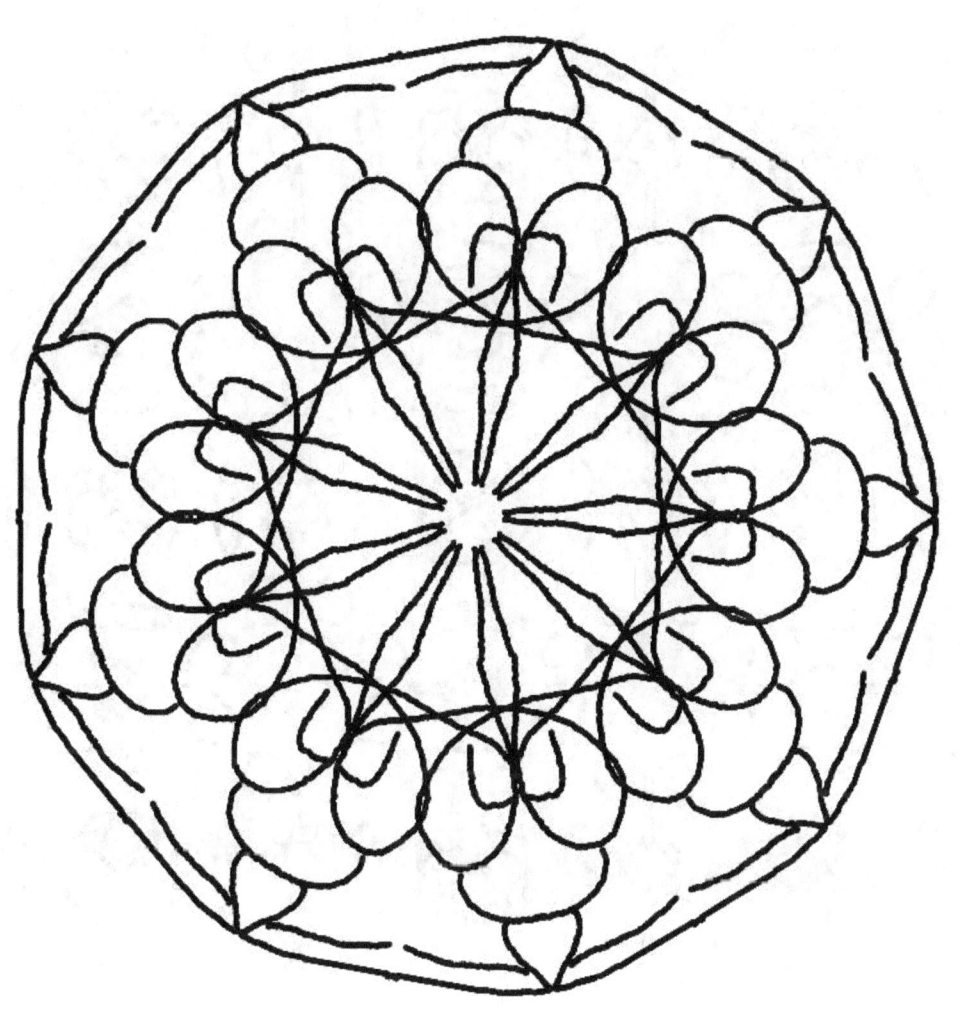

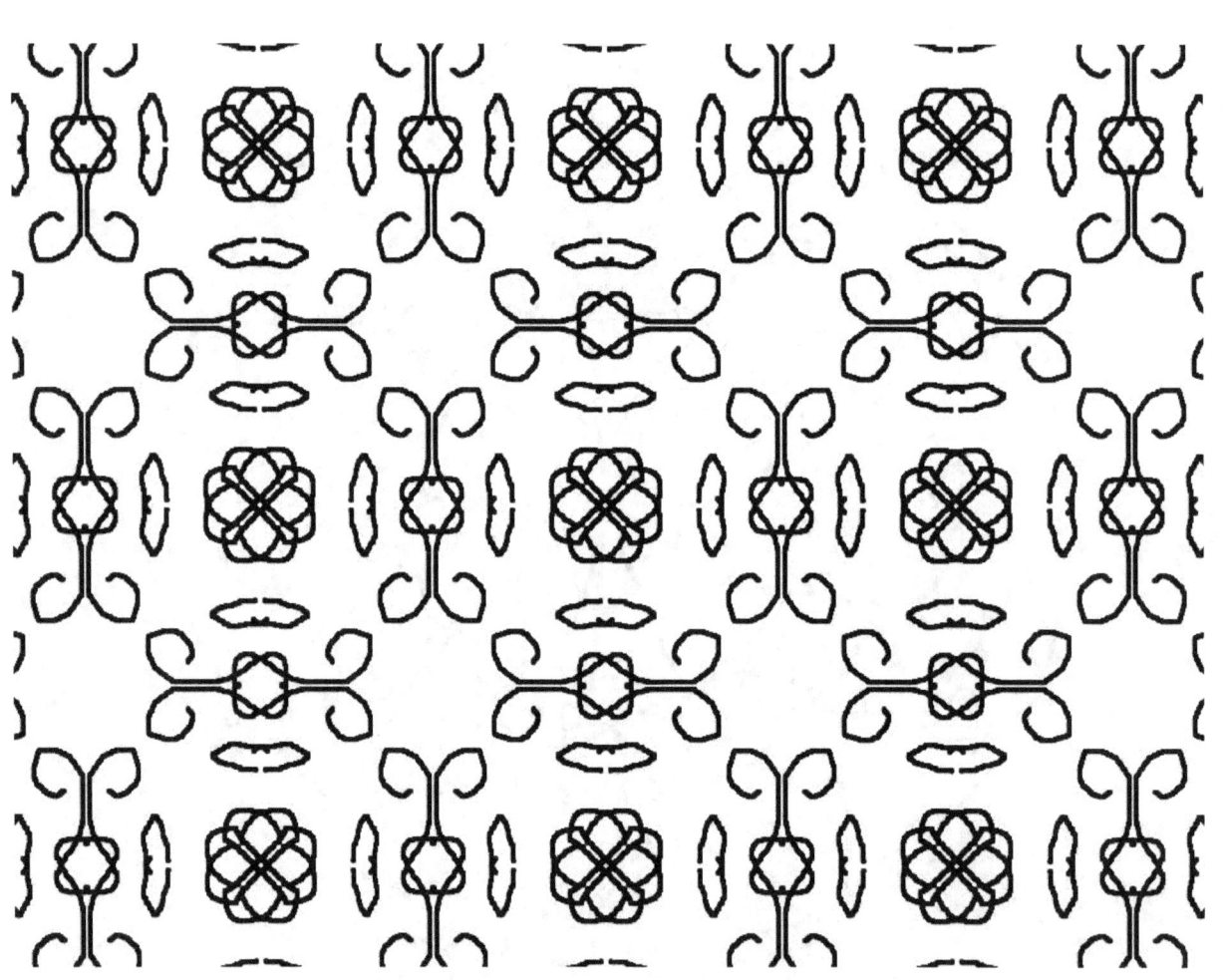

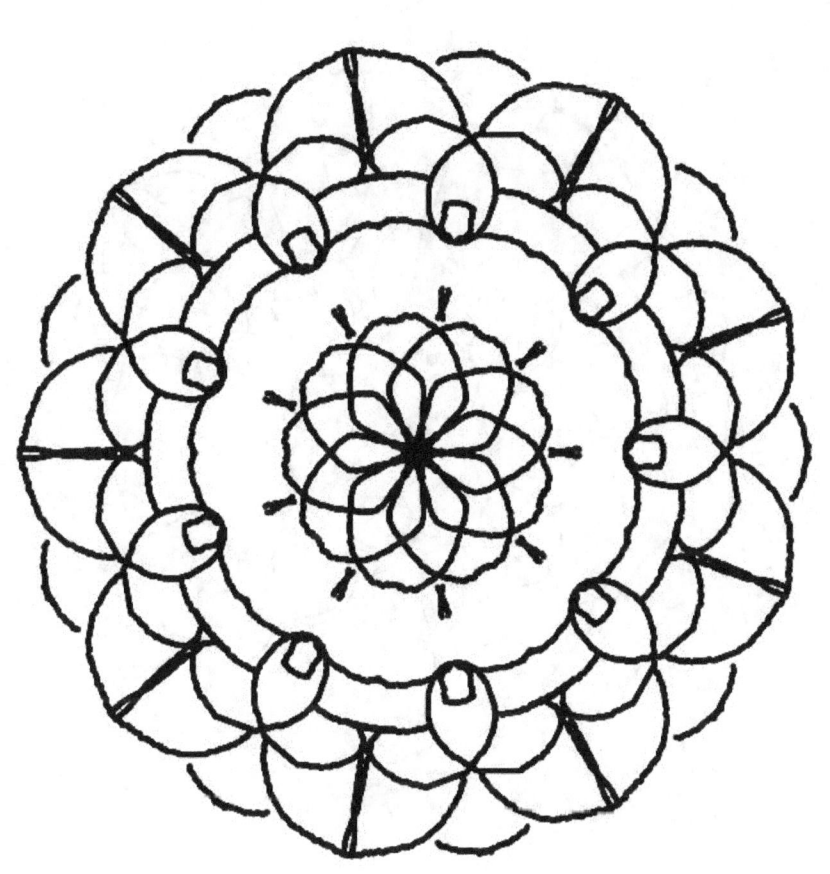

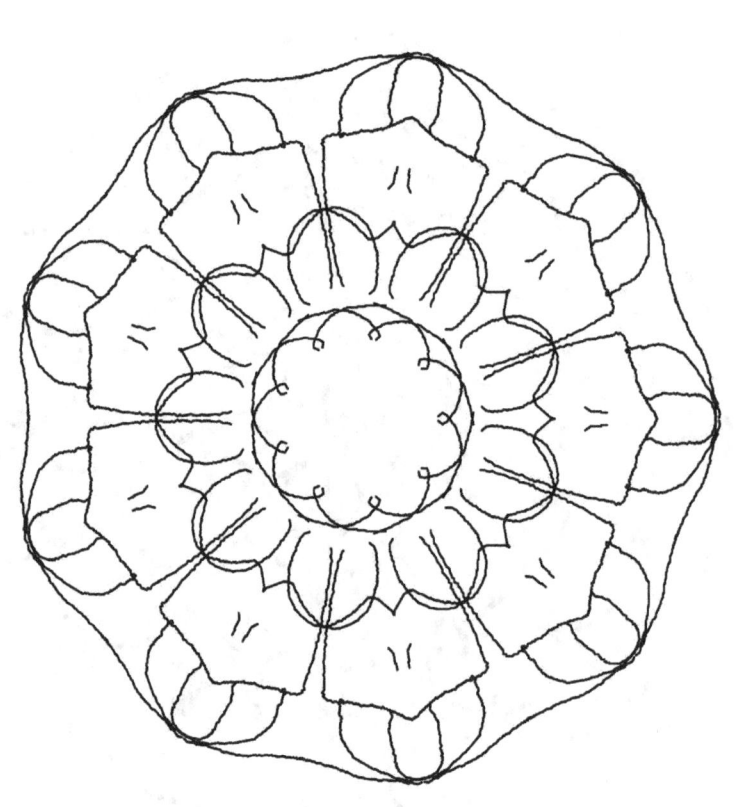

www.ingramcontent.com/pod-product-compliance
Lightning Source LLC
Chambersburg PA
CBHW062238220526
45471CB00009B/3532